# THOMAS AND THE BAD MAN

By Ed. Buck

This was no ordinary day of school for Thomas and his classmates. Thomas began his day just like any other day. Thomas took the bus to school. Thomas gets off the bus and walks to the school gym.

Thomas and his classmates line up on the wall in the gym. The bell rings.  Mrs. Day Thomas's school teacher led Thomas and his classmates to the classroom to start their learning. Thomas learned about reading, writing, numbers, shapes, and colors.

The lunch bell rang. Thomas and his class went to the cafeteria to eat lunch, after lunch recess.  Recess was one of Thomas's favorite parts of the school day. While eating and laughing with Thomas's friend, a bad man with a mask walks in the school.

Thomas sees the bad man in the big picture window. The bad man points something at one of the teachers. Thomas says to Jonathan that looks like my toy gun. Thomas heard a popping sound outside the window. The sound was just like the Fourth of July fireworks. Thomas heard big screams coming from the hallway.

Mrs. Day urgently told her class there is a bad man in our school.

Big danger! Mrs. Day said to her class, do your ABCD for emergencies.

A for Away from the danger, B Be Safe, C Cover Up, D Don't Talk.

Mrs. Day ask Thomas to be her little Hero Helper! Thomas and his classmates quickly moved into an office, to get away from the danger.

Thomas locked the door to be safe. Thomas said don't talk, because we don't want the bad man to hear us.

Thomas and his class did their bad man ABCD's and they were ok and away from the danger until the police came and took the bad man away.

The End

# A.B.C.

- *A- Away from the danger,*

- *B- Be Safe,*

- *C- Cover Up,*

-page intentionally left blank-

-page intentionally left blank-

-page intentionally left blank-

-page intentionally left blank-

-page intentionally left blank-

-page intentionally left blank-

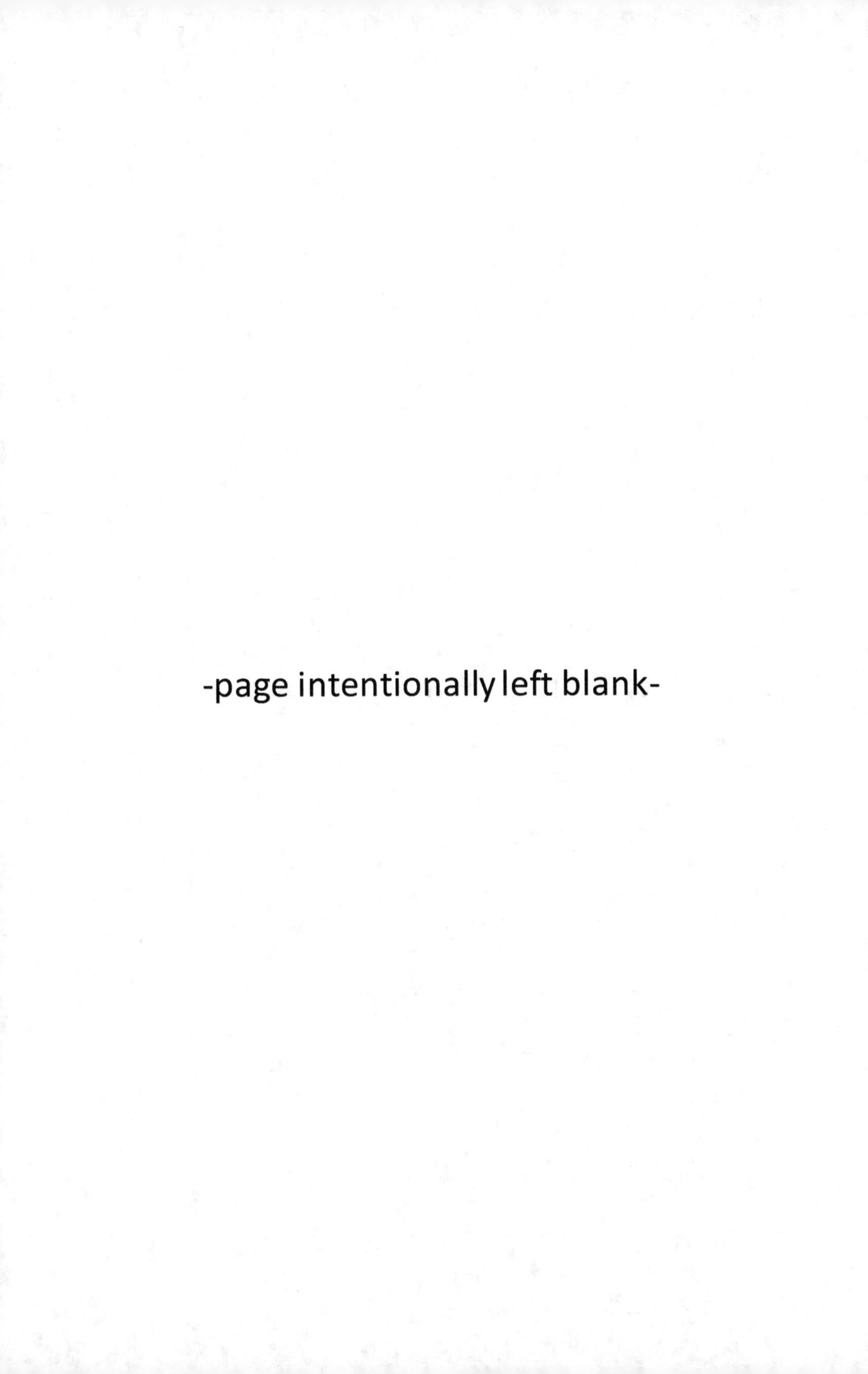

-page intentionally left blank-

-page intentionally left blank-

-page intentionally left blank-

-page intentionally left blank-

-page intentionally left blank-

-page intentionally left blank-

-page intentionally left blank-

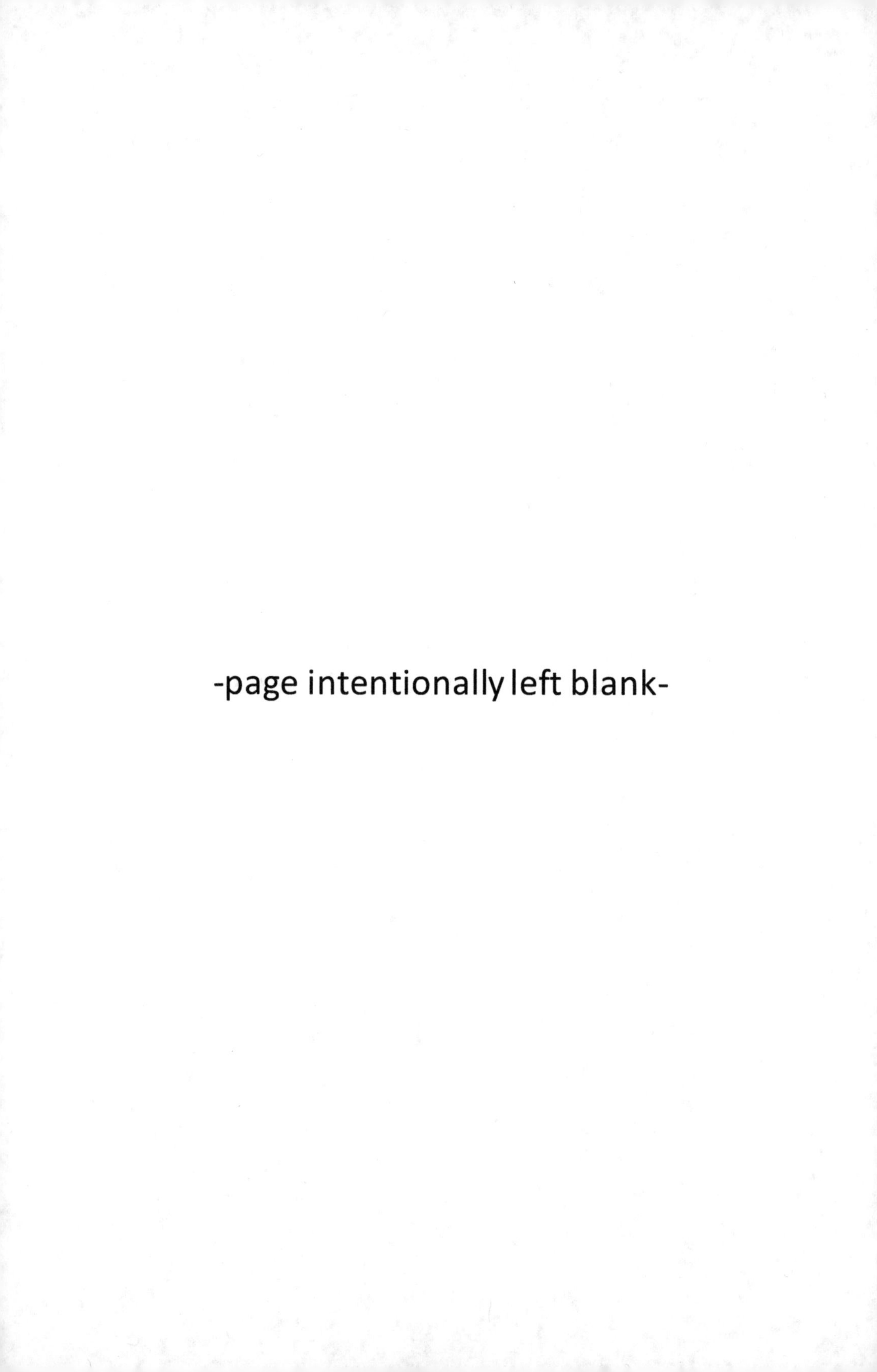

-page intentionally left blank-

-page intentionally left blank-

-page intentionally left blank-